Horsemen of the National Guard.

SAUDI ARABIA

in pictures

by EUGENE GORDON

STERLING PUBLISHING CO., INC. NEW YORK

Oak Tree Press Co., Ltd. London & Sydney

VISUAL GEOGRAPHY SERIES

Alaska
Australia
Austria
Belgium and Luxembourg
Berlin—East and West
Bolivia
Brazil
California
Canada
The Caribbean (English-
    Speaking Islands)
Chile
China
Costa Rica
Cuba
Czechoslovakia
Denmark
Dominican Republic
East Germany
Ecuador
Egypt
El Salvador
England
Ethiopia

Fiji
Finland
Florida
France
Ghana
Greece
Guyana
Haiti
Hawaii
Holland
Honduras
Hong Kong
Hungary
Iceland
India
Indonesia
Iran
Iraq
Ireland
Islands of the
    Mediterranean
Israel
Italy
Ivory Coast

Jamaica
Japan
Jordan
Kenya
Korea
Kuwait
Lebanon
Madagascar (Malagasy)
Malawi
Malaysia and Singapore
Mexico
Nepal
New Zealand
Nigeria
Norway
Pakistan and Bangladesh
Panama and the Canal
    Zone
Paraguay
Peru
The Philippines
Poland
Portugal

Puerto Rico
Rhodesia
Russia
Saudi Arabia
Scotland
Senegal
South Africa
Spain
The Sudan
Sweden
Switzerland
Tahiti and the
    French Islands of
    the Pacific
Taiwan
Thailand
Tunisia
Turkey
Uruguay
The U.S.A.
Venezuela
Wales
West Germany

PICTURE CREDITS

The author and publisher wish to thank the following for use of some photographs in this book: ARAMCO, Dhahran, Saudi Arabia; Inter-Continental Hotels, New York; Burnett H. Moody; NASA, Washington, D.C.; The New York Public Library, New York; Royal Embassy of Saudi Arabia, Washington, D.C.; Saudi Arabian Airlines (Saudia); the United Nations and its specialized agencies: FAO, UNICEF and WHO, New York.

Mecca and the Great Mosque with the Kaaba as they appeared in the 19th century.

CONTENTS

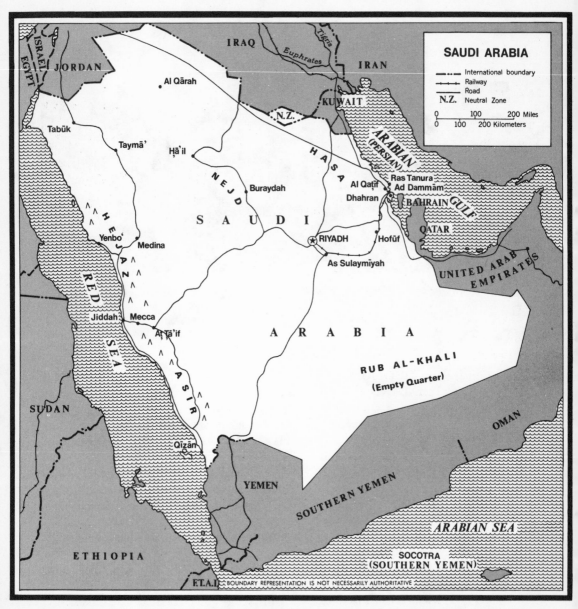

Note: the body of water between Iran and the Arabian Peninsula is called the Arabian Gulf in Arab countries, and the Persian Gulf in other countries.

An aerial view of the desert near the Hofuf Oasis reveals a sculptured effect created by strong winds. The black spots are date groves partially covered by the wind-blown sand.

INTRODUCTION

THE KINGDOM of Saudi Arabia occupies most of the Arabian Peninsula, but the history of this region is more than just the history of a country or a people. It was here that the Semites began to emerge on the stage of recorded history, and here was the birthplace of Mohammed, the prophet who established Islam, one of the world's major religions. It is a huge country, but much of it is an inhospitable sandy desert with little or no rainfall. There is not one river, and in the interior, daytime temperatures of 130° F (54° C) are common, suddenly giving way to the chill of night. It was from here that the first adherents of Islam charged out on their swift horses with the Koran in one hand and the sword in the other to conquer many lands.

Until about 1940 Saudi Arabia had changed little since Biblical times. Then, in the late 1930's, oil was discovered and suddenly the winds of change began to blow in the desert. Much has been altered and much has remained

In the bazaars one can see camel saddles, ancient muskets, aromatic woods and holy water alongside souvenirs of Mecca made in Japan, and Persian prayer rugs made in Italy. A few donkeys along with cars of every type fight the traffic, the car drivers blow musical horns, while the donkey drivers shout to encourage their beasts to move faster. In the background radios blasting with the latest hit song from Cairo blend with the call of the *muezzin*, summoning the faithful to prayer.

The Saudi mechanic who operates an oil well today was most likely a camel driver a few years ago. His cousins probably still live in the desert in goathair tents, with a way of life that has changed very little since the time of Abraham.

In the holy city of Mecca, a hotel was built by European architects, who were nonetheless forbidden to enter the city!

It is these contrasting elements that make up Saudi Arabia.

the same. In settled areas the car has replaced the camel, but the nomadic Bedouin still clings to his ancient ways, forever moving with his goats and camels in search of new grazing land and water.

In Saudi Arabia, a man confronts fried chicken served by a United States fast-food company. A life-size cut-out of the firm's founder appears behind him.

The landscape of the Rub Al-Khali, or Empty Quarter, consists of an almost lifeless desert, 250,000 square miles (650,000 sq km) in area. The characteristic elements of this desert landscape are withered shrubs, dunes and drifting sand.

1. THE LAND

SAUDI ARABIA occupies an area of nearly 900,000 square miles (2,340,000 sq km)—about the size of the United States east of the Mississippi, and somewhat larger than all ten European Common Market countries, plus Spain. On its western coast, running parallel with the Red Sea, is the narrow coastal plain of Tihama. Farther inland, the Hejaz mountains rise to 9,000 feet (2,700 m), then slope gently towards the east, forming a desert plateau with an average elevation of 2,000 to 3,000 feet (600 to 900 m).

The southern part of the country contains the Rub Al-Khali or Empty Quarter, one of the world's most isolated and forbidding terrains. Almost completely waterless and nearly devoid of life, this desert covers an area as large as the state of Texas.

Saudi Arabia is bordered on the west by the Red Sea, on the north by Jordan, Iraq, Kuwait and two Neutral Zones between Iraq and Kuwait. On the east, it is bounded by the Arabian Gulf, the Sheikhdom of Qatar, and the

Abha, the capital of Asir and one of the most scenic spots in the country, is 7,000 feet (2,100 m) above sea level.

United Arab Emirates (formerly called the Seven Trucial Sheikhdoms), and on the south by Yemen, Southern Yemen (formerly called the Aden Protectorate), and Oman. Many of these boundaries are ill-defined and border incidents have occurred, particularly along the frontier with Yemen.

REGIONS

Saudi Arabia is divided into four main geographical areas—Hejaz, Nejd, Hasa and Asir. Hejaz, in the western part of the country, contains the important cities of Mecca, Medina, Jiddah and Taif. Nejd is the central part of the country and contains the capital city of Riyadh. Hasa is frequently referred to as the Eastern Province, and it is here that most of the oil wells are located. Asir, in the southwest part of the country, has the best agricultural land due to heavier rainfall.

A young Jiddah boy is delighted with the dates presented to him during a visit to a date grove on the Mecca road. Date production is still an important source of revenue in the kingdom.

THE OASES

This vast country does not have any rivers or lakes except for *wadis* or river beds that contain water only during the seasonal rains. The only other running waters are small streams

For hundreds of years the Hofuf Oasis has had a sand dune area 20 miles (32 km) long and 5 miles (8 km) wide encroaching on it at the rate of 40 feet (12 m) a year. ARAMCO *has completed a detailed study outlining a series of control measures which will halt the movement of the dunes.*

fed by wells. To a large extent, the country depends for its water on underground sources.

An oasis is an island of greenery in an otherwise barren desert. This fertility is due to the presence of underground water in the form of springs or wells. The amount of water that is available usually determines the size of the oasis. Some consist merely of a few palm trees edging a muddy water-hole, and support no permanent inhabitants, but provide life-giving water for the thirsty traveller. Other oases cover large areas and contain small towns supporting a permanent population of several thousand people, who make a living raising camels, sheep and goats and grow a variety of vegetables and fruits.

Wherever there is enough water to last for the whole year, large scale agriculture is possible. Through irrigation, the government is creating many artificial oases to encourage the people in the area to settle down and grow their own food.

CLIMATE

The Arabian Peninsula is a part of the great desert belt that stretches across Africa from Morocco in the west to Pakistan's Indus Valley in central Asia in the east. Along with the other countries of this belt, Saudi Arabia has a very dry, hot climate with frequent dust- and sandstorms. During the day the summer temperatures can rise to 130°F (54°C) dropping to about 40 to 50°F (4 to 10°C) at night. It is not so hot along the coasts of the Red Sea and Arabian Gulf, but the humidity is much higher, particularly on the Arabian Gulf, known for its frequent heavy fogs.

In the central and northern parts of the country, temperatures drop below freezing in the winter, but snowfall occurs only at the highest altitudes. Riyadh is quite cool in the winter, with daytime temperatures dropping as low as 50°F (10°C).

The average rainfall is 3 to 5 inches (7.5 to 12.5 cm) annually, with the Asir region in the southwest getting the greatest amount, about 10 to 20 inches (25 to 50 cm) a year.

FLORA

The vegetation is generally very sparse due to lack of rain and the high salt content of the soil. True trees are rare—in most areas non-existent, while small shrubs and annual herbs are common. Most plants have had to adapt to the conditions of desert existence, some by reducing the leaf surface area—spiny or needle-like

Trees grow in the mountains of Asir, where rainfall is more abundant than elsewhere in Saudi Arabia.

In a small town in the southern province of Asir, the dome-shaped houses are thatched with reeds.

leaves lose less water from evaporation. Others have acquired the ability to store water, and some have developed a tolerance for salty water.

Among small trees and shrubs adapted to the desert climate are the aloe and tamarisk, found all over the country. In the higher altitudes are figs, carobs, and junipers, as well as cactus-like euphorbias.

Wild flowers are abundant in the higher elevations, particularly during the rainy season. Reeds grow in isolated areas where the water supply permits it, and are used by the people to build huts and to thatch roofs.

The most important cultivated plant is the date palm. The date fruit is a popular food, while the tree supplies valuable wood and other by-products. The palm leaves are used for thatching roofs.

FAUNA

Wild animals include two antelopes—the small, fleet-footed gazelle and the large, stately oryx (now close to extinction). The carnivores are represented by the fox, lynx, wolf, hyena, wildcat, cheetah, jackal and an occasional leopard. Smaller mammals include the hedgehog, hare and hyrax.

Locusts used to be so numerous as to constitute a plague. Curiously, they were also esteemed as food by some of the Bedouins. There are many other species of insects, snakes, lizards, and scorpions, and the coastal waters contain many varieties of fish.

Ostriches are thought to be extinct, but flamingoes and pelicans are common, along with many other shore birds. The most common bird in the oases is the bulbul, and this songbird figures often in the popular poetry of the country.

No mention of the animal life of Saudi Arabia would be complete without a word on the camel and the horse, although both of these are domestic, not wild, animals.

THE CAMEL

The most important animal in the history of Saudi Arabia is the camel, which has made travel possible in the barren and frequently waterless desert. The camel of Arabia is the single-humped variety, or dromedary, as opposed to the two-humped camel of Central Asia, the Bactrian. The dromedary has flat, broad, thick-soled, cloven hoofs that do not sink in sand. Because camels have the ability to go for days without water, and longer, if provided with

11

Bedouins and their camels camp near an oil drilling rig in eastern Saudi Arabia.

juicy plants, they are especially adapted to desert life.

Camels have been observed to drink as much as 30 gallons (114 litres) of water at one time. Capable of carrying loads of from 250 to 600 pounds (1,125 to 2,700 kilos) depending on the season and availability of water, they can travel 20 to 30 miles (32 to 48 km) a day. The milk of the camel forms an important part in the diet of the desert Arab, often being the only liquid that the nomadic Bedouin has access to.

A lightweight camel used only for riding is also raised.

Traditionally the camel has been a popular subject in the literature and folklore of Arabia, which have endowed the animal with mythical

The Arabian Horse is famous the world over for its speed and graceful lines.

Offshore drilling platforms, operated by ARAMCO, *obtain oil from the sea bottom. Much of the oil in Saudi Arabia comes from offshore wells.*

qualities of beauty, wisdom, endurance, and other highly desirable traits. Travellers to the desert who are not so romantically inclined have found the camel to be an ill-tempered beast that often bites, kicks and spits.

THE ARABIAN HORSE

The horse was introduced from the north ages ago and in the isolation of Arabia, a distinctive breed developed. The small, handsome Arabian horse has great stamina and speed, and is an ancestor of the Thoroughbred horse of the West.

The horse, like the camel, has played a very important part in the history of Arabia, for it was this animal that provided speedy transportation in the 7th century, when the Arabs set out on their famous conquests. For the Bedouin it was the perfect steed for making raids upon other tribes or desert travellers. Unable to compete with the camel, the horse was never used for long journeys through the desert, however. Today the horse is a status symbol in Arabia—only the wealthy can afford the price and upkeep of a good one.

NATURAL RESOURCES

Saudi Arabia has one great natural resource—petroleum. In the remote past, hundreds of millions of years ago, the Arabian Gulf extended over a larger area than it does today. The seas at one time covered much of the land mass east, west, and north of the Persian Gulf, including eastern and northern Saudi Arabia, Kuwait,

Oil prospectors set up camp in the Rub Al-Khali.

Efforts are being made for development of water resources. Here a newly constructed well provides badly needed water.

and parts of Iran. In time the land gradually rose, the Gulf shrank, and large areas of what had been sea bottom became dry land.

During the time that this land was under the sea, vast quantities of dead plant and animal life were deposited on the sea bottom. This organic material was slowly changed by geological processes into a mineral oil—petroleum.

The Gulf area contains perhaps the world's largest single deposits of oil.

Diving for pearls is still carried on in the Arabian Gulf, whose waters were formerly one of the main sources of pearls. However, in the last few decades, pearl fishing has decreased considerably, due to competition from the cultured pearl industry in Japan.

14

The Holy Kaaba in Mecca is covered with a richly embroidered dark curtain. Mecca is the place toward which all Muslims face when praying. In the background some of the buildings of the old part of the city itself can be seen.

OTHER RESOURCES

As a result of the development of oil, several other important resources have been created—petrochemicals, fertilizers, and liquid propane gas. Studies have shown that other minerals such as copper, manganese, silver, gypsum, and sulphur—can be profitably exploited. In 1939, a mining company was formed to work the ancient gold and silver mine at Mahad Al-Dahab, not far from Medina. This mine was in use in the days of King Solomon. After 1954, operations ceased because it was no longer profitable to run the mine.

After 1970, concessions were granted to several United States and European firms to explore the country for minerals.

Pearl fishing is carried on in the Arabian Gulf area, but only on a small scale.

CITIES

MECCA

The religious capital of the country and the most sacred city for all Muslims, Mecca is the birthplace of the prophet Mohammed and the site of the Great Mosque, towards which all Muslims face five times each day when praying. It is the spiritual hub of Islam, the religion of the Muslims (or Moslems).

Mecca has a population of 367,000 people and is located in the province of Hejaz in a dry rocky valley surrounded by hills. Due to the hot, dry climate of the area, there are few agricultural settlements near the city and, except for the manufacturing of religious articles, there is little local industry.

From early antiquity Mecca was crisscrossed by important caravan routes, thus making it an important market town. Even before Islam, the

15

A group of pilgrims wearing the traditional pilgrim's garb face the Holy Kaaba in the courtyard of the Great Mosque.

city was the sacred place of a cult of idol worshippers. Today Mecca owes its prosperity entirely to the pilgrim trade. Several hundreds of thousands of pilgrims come annually, and the housing, feeding and servicing of these people is a gigantic enterprise in which the Government lends a helping hand by organizing transportation and the distribution of supplies.

The Great Mosque which dominates much of the city, dates from the 8th century, but has been constantly enlarged. Presently it can accommodate 300,000 pilgrims; on the outside

A familiar sight to the pilgrim is the main entrance of the Great Mosque in Mecca. Behind this ornate façade is a vast courtyard where the Holy Kaaba is housed.

Medina is the second sacred city after Mecca. Seen here at night is the section of the "suk" (market) where the food vendors are concentrated. Large quantities of meats, vegetables, and other spicy and fragrant foods permeate the air with their pungent aromas.

there is parking space for 4,000 vehicles. Mecca also houses a College of Education and the Sharia or Islamic Studies College.

Mecca the Blessed, as it is called by Muslims, has been ruled by many tribes and sects, but the most prominent among them was the Koreish tribe. It was from this tribe that Mohammed was descended. After the death of Mohammed, the members of the Koreish were afforded many privileges and were granted the honorary title of Sherif. The highest personage was the Grand Sherif, the ruler of Mecca. Most of the Grand Sherifs came from one of the most distinguished families, the Beni Hashem or Hashemites. The Hashemites ruled Mecca, with some interruptions, until 1924, when Ibn Saud overthrew them and proclaimed himself king.

MEDINA

Second sacred city, after Mecca, Medina has 200,000 people and is located in a flourishing oasis, growing great quantities of dates, fruits, and grains.

The main building is the Great Mosque, also known as the Prophet's Mosque, which contains the tombs of Mohammed, his daughter Fatimah, and the Caliph Omar, who is revered by Muslims for having laid down the legal and administrative principles of Islam. Medina also houses the Islamic University, an important school for Islamic studies, and nearby is the famous Medina Library, a treasure house of Arabic texts on religion, geography, and medicine. The most valued and cherished book in this library is a Koran, handwritten on parchment, dating from the 7th century.

17

An old house in Jiddah is decorated with classic arabesque designs executed in plaster. Geometric designs are the only decorations permitted by the Koran.

Before the flight (Hegira) of Mohammed to Medina in A.D. 622, the city was called Yathrib. After the arrival of Mohammed, the city began to grow in importance and eventually became the seat of the caliphate, or Muslim leadership. It began to lose its importance in 662, when the caliphate was transferred to the more centrally located Damascus. Constant fighting among the local tribes resulted in frequent changes of rule. Eventually Medina was occupied by the Mamelukes from Egypt, then by the Ottoman (Turkish) Empire in 1517. The Saudis took it from the Turks in 1804 only to lose it to them again in 1812. It remained part of the Ottoman Empire until the end of World War I, when Ibn Saud consolidated his rule over all Hejaz.

JIDDAH

Situated on the Red Sea with a population of 600,000, Jiddah is the country's most important seaport. The inhabitants are of varied ethnic backgrounds—Arabs, Persians, Negroes, Indians, and people of other races, too, for most of the foreign embassies are located in this city.

Rugs and religious articles are manufactured locally, but the biggest industry is the handling of pilgrims. About 90 per cent of all the pilgrims from foreign lands enter Saudi Arabia through Jiddah. They used to come by boat, but, in increasingly larger numbers, they now come by air.

Jiddah has the country's largest bazaar (market place), filled with the exotic products and spices of the Orient alongside the assembly-line goods of Japan, Germany, and the United States. Outside the city, near the Medina Gate, is the site of the reputed grave of Eve. Once about 200 feet (60 m) long and 10 feet (3 m) high, it was demolished in 1927 by the Wahhabi sect.

RIYADH

Riyadh is the largest city, the political and administrative capital of the country and the heart of the Wahhabi reform movement. With a population of about 660,000, it is situated in the Nejd region, in a well watered fertile valley lush with date groves, orchards, and fields of grain. Riyadh, connected with the Dhahran on the Arabian Gulf by a railway, has a modern airport, and is important for the manufacture of cement, plastics, and prefabricated houses. The Riyadh University has faculties in the arts, sciences, religion, commerce, agriculture, pharmacy, engineering and medicine. Also

Fast-growing Riyadh is a city of broad avenues and open spaces.

located in Riyadh are the Royal Vocational Institute, the Military College, the Air Force College and the Interior Security Forces College.

The city is surrounded by a number of villages and towns rich in palm groves. These communities provide most of Riyadh's requirements in fruits and vegetables.

DHAHRAN

This oil camp in the Eastern Province, with about 45,000 people, is a very important link in the country's oil exploration and development. The headquarters of the Arabian American Oil Company (called ARAMCO) is here. Dhahran has a busy international airport and is connected to Hofuf and Riyadh by a railway and linked by pipe lines with Ras Tanura and other important oil hubs. The area has grown up since 1938, an island of modernity in the middle of the desert, full of air-conditioned prefabricated houses and supermarkets. A College of Petroleum and Mineral Resources has been set up in Dhahran.

The present city of Jiddah is about 300 years old. Twelve miles (19 km) to the south is the site of the old city of Jiddah, founded in the 7th century A.D.

Dammam, the most important port city on the Arabian Gulf and the capital of the Eastern Province, has a population of about 128,000.

DAMMAM

Dammam is a commercial city of 128,000 people and the most important port on the Arabian Gulf. The local industries are based on fishing, agriculture, stock raising and oil operations.

TAIF

Located in central Hejaz at an altitude of 5,000 feet (1,500 m), Taif is blessed with a mild climate and serves as the country's chief summer resort. Here, many of Saudi Arabia's notables have luxurious villas surrounded by lush gardens. Taif is in the middle of an important orchard region producing much of the fruit of Hejaz. Taif is also famous for its superior attar of roses, an important item, for the pilgrims use it to scent the ritual water with which they wash themselves. The population of Taif is well over 200,000.

HOFUF

Hofuf lies in the largest oasis in Hasa province and is an important agricultural and commercial town, linked with Riyadh to the west and Dhahran to the east by railway. Hofuf raises large quantities of dates, vegetables, fruits and barley and has many small cottage industries producing textiles and copper and brass handicrafts.

AL-KHOBAR

Nothing but a few mud huts in 1958, Al-Khobar is today a thriving city with running water, sewers, and traffic jams. The population is a mixture of Arabs, Indians, Europeans, and Americans.

VILLAGES

Small villages ordinarily consist of densely packed groups of houses surrounded by orchards and fields and frequently by a mud wall. Each house often has a small garden or orchard of its own. Beyond the fields and orchards on the outskirts of the village are the grazing lands. The larger and older villages are generally built around a *suk* or bazaar where the periodic markets are held. The bazaar also serves as a gathering place for special occasions, and is usually located close to the village mosque.

Oil money, however, is transforming some traditional villages. One example is Jubail, a coastal village north of Dhahran, which is being developed as an industrial port city, producing fertilizer, petrochemicals, steel and aluminium.

In 1977, King Khalid, in the presence of officials of the Saudi Arabian government and ARAMCO, inaugurated the Berri Natural Gas Liquids Center, built to produce fuel, chemical feedstock and export gas liquids.

2. HISTORY

FOR THOUSANDS of years the Arabian Peninsula had been the home of nomadic Semitic tribes, some of whom established settlements in the oases and along the more important caravan routes.

Southern Arabia (Yemen and Southern Yemen) was for a long time the prime source of frankincense and myrrh which were used in large quantities by the Romans and the Egyptians for religious purposes, embalming and cosmetics. Other important commodities traded and carried north by the nomadic merchants of Arabia included silk and spices from India, ivory, animal skins and slaves from Africa, and semi-precious stones, gold, and possibly copper, from Arabia itself. Starting from southern and western Arabia a network of important caravan routes crisscrossed the peninsula eventually ending in Egypt, Palestine, Syria and Babylonia.

The early inhabitants of what is now Saudi Arabia performed the important rôle of middlemen between southern Arabia with its precious commodities and the densely settled areas

Mount Arafat and the pilgrim camp appeared this way to Sir Richard Burton during his visit in 1853.

BURTON

Another famous explorer to visit Mecca and Medina was the Englishman, Sir Richard Burton. In 1853, disguised as a pilgrim under the name of Al-Hajj-Abdullah, he arrived at Jiddah, then proceeded to Mecca and Medina to complete the pilgrimage, all the while making detailed notes of everything he saw. His diary was later published and to this day it is one of the best descriptions of life and customs in Arabia.

DOUGHTY

Charles M. Doughty spent two years travelling with the Bedouins of Arabia from 1875 until 1877. His book "Travels in Arabia Deserta" is ranked among the best travel books ever written. Due to its ponderous style, it is not easy reading, but those willing to give it the attention it deserves will be rewarded with a rich panorama of desert life.

PHILBY

H. St. John Philby, British explorer and diplomat, was born in Ceylon and came to Arabia in 1915. He eventually became a close friend and adviser to King Ibn Saud. Philby became a Muslim and spent close to 40 years in Arabia

Sir Richard Burton, the English adventurer and traveller, visited Mecca and Medina in 1853 disguised as a Muslim pilgrim.

during which time he explored and studied the country in greater depth than anyone else, writing about a dozen books on the subject.

THESIGER

Wilfred Thesiger, British explorer, was born in Ethiopia in 1910, grew up in Africa and came

The city of Medina appeared like this in the early 19th century, as seen by an Arab artist of the period.

to Arabia in 1945 to head a team of specialists investigating the plague-like periodic movements of the locusts, which were suspected of originating in the Empty Quarter of Arabia.

Eventually he crossed the Empty Quarter disguised as a Bedouin. Barefoot and with a few Arab companions, he travelled through much of that area. His descriptions of life in the desert are unique, due to his almost mystical affinity for the primitive way of life of the Bedouin.

THE WAHHABIS AND THE SAUDI DYNASTY

Saudi Arabia became for the first time a distinct political unit in the late 18th century when the religious reformer, Abdul-Wahhab, under the patronage of the Saudi dynasty of Nejd, embarked upon unifying the country and reforming and purifying Islam.

The Saudis encountered the hostility of the Turks and Egyptians, and in 1818 the Turkish and Egyptian forces invaded and occupied Nejd. The Egyptians were unable to maintain control and the Saudis returned to power in 1824.

A period of strife between Arab factions forced the Saudi dynasty into exile, when another family, the Rashids, won control of Riyadh.

The modern history of Saudi Arabia starts in 1902, when Abd Al-Aziz Al Saud, known in the outside world as Ibn Saud, left Kuwait,

25

A public square in Jiddah appeared like this about 125 years ago. Since then Jiddah has become the main commercial city of the country, but many of these ancient buildings still remain in the old quarter of the city.

where the Saud family was living in exile. With a handful of followers, he recaptured the family's traditional capital, Riyadh, from the Rashids. By 1914, Ibn Saud had reconquered most of the provinces of Nejd and Hasa and was recognized as Emir of Nejd by the British during World War I. During this war the walls of the Ottoman Empire were crumbling and the Turks were losing their grip over the Middle East, setting the stage for the independence of Arabia.

The British were sympathetic to Ibn Saud because of his harassment of the Turks, but they gave most of their support to his rival, the Emir Hussein, ruler of Hejaz. With the aid of the famous English adventurer, Lawrence of Arabia, the Emir Hussein was induced to revolt against the Turks by the British. Hussein then declared himself King of Hejaz, but was subsequently defeated by Ibn Saud, who by 1925 consolidated his rule over Hejaz.

SAUDI ARABIA ESTABLISHED

In 1926, Ibn Saud was proclaimed King of Hejaz and Sultan of Nejd. In 1932, the two areas were united into the Kingdom of Saudi Arabia. The imposing figure of Ibn Saud began to dominate as he ended the tribal divisions of the country. He established a firm, autocratic rule and by strictly enforcing the laws, he ensured the safety of the pilgrims travelling to Mecca and Medina, thus gradually forging a unified country.

OIL TRANSFORMS THE DESERT

In 1933, King Ibn Saud granted an oil concession to the California-Arabian Oil Company, later to become the Arabian American Oil Company (ARAMCO). The first important well was discovered in 1938 and major production started shortly after World War II.

26

This early 19th-century engraving depicts the camel-borne litter of Arabia called the "taktarawan." This strange conveyance formerly served to transport people of high class only, but it is no longer in use.

Barely 25 years later, the huge incomes from oil royalties had brought about incredible changes. A country that existed in almost complete isolation from the outside world was transformed within two decades into a country with jet airports, television stations, and diesel trucks in place of camels.

This rapid transformation took its toll. King Ibn Saud himself lived an austere life, but the plentiful easy money pouring into the country was often mismanaged. In 1953, he died at the age of 73, and was followed on the throne by his eldest son, King Saud Ibn Abd Al-Aziz, who exercised direct rule until 1958 and then again from 1960 to 1962.

The traditional, simple garb of the pilgrim contrasts with that of the veiled woman. This engraving was made almost 150 years ago.

The late Ibn Saud founded the Kingdom of Saudi Arabia in 1932 by uniting Hejaz and Nejd. Here the ruler of Bahrain, Sheikh Hamab Al-Khalifah is on his left.

In early 1958, King Saud's rule was interrupted by chaotic financial conditions at home due to reckless spending, and strained relations with President Nasser of Egypt. The Royal Family convinced King Saud to delegate the direct running of the government to his younger but more efficient brother, Feisal. In 1960, Saud took back full control, but in 1962 poor health coupled with internal pressures for reform and external pressures generated by Egyptian propaganda, and Saud's involvement on the royalist side in the Yemen war, forced the King to delegate powers again to Feisal.

In 1964, Crown Prince Feisal assumed complete authority and on November 2 of the same year he was proclaimed king by the senior members of the royal family and religious leaders. Saud subsequently died in exile in 1969. King Feisal, who had been born in 1906, from an early age showed administrative ability. In 1925, he was appointed Viceroy of Hejaz and in 1930, he was given the post of Foreign Minister. King Feisal travelled widely and through the years visited the United States, Iran, Kuwait, Jordan, Pakistan, Spain, Turkey, Morocco, Mali, Tunisia and many other countries.

THE EMBARGO

King Feisal assumed a new rôle in world politics in 1973 after the outbreak of war between Israel and the Arab nations of Egypt and Syria in October of that year. The king until then had refrained from serious involvement in the Middle East situation, although he was under pressure from the leaders of other Arab states to use Saudi oil as a political weapon. These leaders called for an embargo on Arab oil shipment to nations giving support to Israel. Feisal gave in after the 1973 war began and agreed to cut down oil shipments to the West. Then, when President Nixon indicated his intention of stepping up the flow of arms to Israel, Feisal cut off all Saudi oil to the United States. He was joined in this move by the other Arab oil-producing nations, causing an energy crisis among the industrial nations, some of whom, like Japan and the Western European countries were heavily dependent on Arab oil. Most of these countries were forced to change their stand on the Arab-Israeli conflict. The United States, much less dependent on Arab oil, held out, along with the Netherlands.

Then, following the negotiation of a cease-fire between Israel and its opponents by U.S. Secretary of State Henry Kissinger, the embargo came to an end in March, 1974, pending further working out of details. Whatever the outcome, Saudi Arabia had taken the decisive measure of using its vast oil resources as a political weapon.

RECENT EVENTS

In March, 1975, King Feisal was assassinated by a young prince of the Saudi royal family who had a record of instability. The King's brother, Crown Prince Khalid, succeeded to the throne. The assassin was later beheaded in public according to Saudi custom. No important policy changes were made by the new King.

The market in the city of Buraidah, northwest of Riyadh, is a busy place. Buraidah started out as an oasis but grew to become an important commercial city.

3. THE PEOPLE

THE POPULATION of Saudi Arabia was about 7,000,000, according to a census that was conducted in 1974. Unofficial estimates placed it as high as 9,000,000 in 1979. About 90 per cent of the population is pure Arab, descendants of the native Arab tribes with some admixture of Negro blood from slaves imported from Africa over the centuries.

Along the Arabian Gulf there are some inhabitants of Iranian and Pakistani descent, but otherwise the population is homogeneous, both in language and religion. The main division is between the settled people and those who are nomadic, the Bedouins. These two groups have traditionally been antagonistic to each other.

Until recently a large proportion of the

A page from the Koran containing a "sura" (chapter) is decorated on the borders with typical arabesque and geometric designs. The Koran explicitly forbids the making of pictures depicting human beings or any other living forms.

THE PILGRIMAGE

The burning desire and ambition of every Muslim is to make the pilgrimage to Mecca. Muslims from the four corners of the earth gather each year to make this sacred journey. During the pilgrimage, all social and political differences are temporarily laid aside. Every pilgrim, whether beggar, prince, wealthy land-lord, or poor camel-driver, wears the same simple white garment and participates in the same rituals. However, some arrive in Mecca in air-conditioned Cadillacs, others are crowded into huge trucks or buses, and still others arrive on foot after walking for days.

The first goal of the pilgrims is the Kaaba, a large structure in the shape of a cube. In one corner of the wall, set in a silver frame, is the sacred black stone. Legend has it that the original structure was built by Abraham, but was subsequently destroyed and rebuilt several times. The building is covered with heavy dark curtains, embroidered with verses from the Koran. It is towards the Kaaba that all Muslims turn five times each day when praying.

During the pilgrimage each pilgrim has to circle the Kaaba seven times. The sick and crippled are carried on litters. The following day the pilgrims' next goal is the plain of Arafat, about 12 miles (19 km) from Mecca. Here they

Pilgrims arrive at the airport in Jiddah.

The Holy Kaaba rises above a sea of the faithful. In the foreground, two pilgrims sit in an archway of the Great Mosque's tower.

Pilgrimage City—hundreds of thousands of Muslim pilgrims encamp annually on the plains adjacent to Mount Arafat and the city of Mina, near Mecca. Each year Saudi Arabia is host to approximately 250,000 Muslims who make the Hajj (pilgrimage) to Mecca. The Hajj is one of the five pillars of the Islamic faith, but only those Muslims who are financially and physically able are required to make the journey.

congregate in vast numbers, waiting for the roar of the cannon at sunset, signalling them to proceed to the town of Mina, about five miles away. At Mina are the three white pillars believed to mark the place where Abraham was tempted by the devil as he was about to sacrifice his son to God. Each pilgrim then hurls seven stones at the white pillars, enacting the ceremony called "stoning the devil."

When Abraham was about to sacrifice his son, God replaced the son with a ram, according to scripture. This symbolic sacrifice survives to this day, when tens of thousands of sheep and a smaller number of cattle and camels are slaughtered yearly. Half are butchered in special slaughterhouses set up for this purpose, while the others are killed where they stand in the valley, often right next to the pilgrim's tent. The owner reserves a choice cut of meat for himself, and distributes the rest among the poor.

The valley is a scene of feverish activity—animals being offered for sale by their owners, and butchers and knife sharpeners loudly offering their services amid the cries of the animals. Whatever meat is not consumed is preserved by drying it in the fierce heat of the sun, by a special group of workers from Mecca. Some of the dry meat is carried home by foreign pilgrims as a sacred keepsake.

One of the most common health hazards dur-

A pilgrim to Mecca suffering from heat prostration (one of many) is treated by being dipped in a tub of ice water.

ing the pilgrimage is heat prostration. The government has mobile ambulance units where the affected pilgrim is plunged into a bathtub of cold water, and then transferred to a temporary hospital for additional treatment. All along the pilgrim's route free ice-water is available, and he is encouraged to consume large quantities, to prevent dehydration. A sign of the changing times—the thirsty pilgrim can now purchase ice cream and soft drinks.

The shrine of Al-Safa is one of the required stops for the pilgrims. Here they recite certain prayers in a soft voice, after which they praise God three times, then start to trot (not walk) to the next shrine.

Muslims pray under the graceful arches of the Great Mosque in Mecca. Built in the 8th century, the mosque is constantly being enlarged.

THE WAHHABIS

The Wahhabis were a reform movement founded by Muhammed Ibn Abdul Wahhab who lived in the middle of the 18th century in Ayaina, near Riyadh. By all accounts it seems that he displayed strong religious tendencies even as a youth. It is said that by the time he was 10 he knew the whole Koran by heart, at the ripe age of 12 he was married, and at 14 completed his pilgrimage to Mecca.

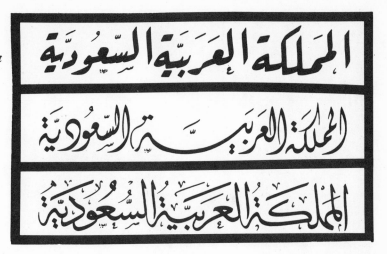

Arabic letters have different forms. The row on the top is for everyday use, the row in the middle is a highly stylized and ornamental version, and the row on the bottom is a highly decorated style used for headlines and titles.

At that time most of the Bedouins took religion rather lightly and Ibn Abdul Wahhab made it his mission to return the people of Arabia to strict observance of the Koran and to bring back the strong penalties introduced by Mohammed against those who did not observe the religious rules. The present ruling family still adheres firmly to the Wahhabi creed, but with less emphasis on some of the stricter aspects.

LANGUAGE

Throughout the country, Arabic is spoken. There are local dialects, but these are minor and do not prevent people from different parts of the country from understanding each other. Arabic is a Semitic language related to Hebrew and Aramaic. The written language is cursive, that is, written in flowing, rounded and connected characters and is read from right to left.

EDUCATION

The literacy rate is about 30 per cent. In the past, many of the people, particularly the Bedouins and those who lived in small villages, never saw any book other than the Koran, and sometimes not even that. To provide education to many is one of the government's main challenges.

Schooling is free and is provided on three levels—elementary, intermediate and secondary

An instructor of chemistry conducts a class of first-year students at the College of Engineering, Riyadh.

A fountain graces the campus of the College of Petroleum and Mineral Resources in Dhahran.

—and there are also commercial, agricultural and vocational schools. Co-education does not exist—boys and girls attend separate schools. Adults without previous education can enroll in night school for a four-year course to qualify them for an elementary educational certificate. The first two years are devoted entirely to teaching them to read and write.

In 1978, Saudi Arabia had 3,597 schools with a total enrolment of 805,000 students. There are 34 teacher training schools and four commercial schools. The country is divided into 23 administrative educational districts.

The Agricultural Department of Riyadh University, with advice from the Food and Agriculture Organization and the help of private consultants, has established a model agriculture project. The Royal Vocational Institute in Riyadh can accommodate 8,000 students in two shifts and has provisions for boarding students.

The University of Riyadh, founded in 1957, has faculties in the arts, sciences, commerce, pharmacy, agriculture, engineering, education, and medicine. There is also a University in Jiddah, which has two faculties in Mecca, and the Islamic University in Medina. In 1963, a College of Petroleum and Mineral Resources was established in Dhahram to develop trained personnel for the country's most important industry, oil.

Students and teachers leave one of the college buildings in Riyadh as classes end.

LITERATURE

In pre-Islamic Arabia, poetry and literature reached its highest form of expression. After Mohammed and the coming of Islam, poetic expression changed, as Mohammed did not approve of the easy-going and romantic poetry common during that time.

A traditional street scene is the subject of this painting by Saudi Arabian artist, Safiya bin Zagr.

The literature of Arabia is full of stories and poems extolling the virtues of romantic love, heroes, war, and the beauty and intelligence of Arabian horses and camels. Poetry and story-telling are ways to hand down a country's history and traditions in a land where most of the population is illiterate.

The best stories and poems were translated into English by 19th-century travellers and scholars, but they do not take well to translation and seem overly ornate, flowery, and without much content. Like everything else in Arabia, literature is dominated by the Koran. In it, poetic expression reached an unsurpassed majestic quality.

It should be noted that part of the literature in the Arabic language did not originate in Arabia itself, but in the highly advanced countries conquered by the Arabs.

LIBRARIES

Mecca, Medina, Riyadh, and Jiddah have a number of libraries. As the holy places of Islam, Mecca and Medina have accumulated through the centuries a priceless collection of manuscripts and printed books—many of them the only ones in existence. Medina has the largest and most important collection, while the best private collection is in Jiddah.

MUSIC AND ART

According to a strict interpretation of the Koran, music is not allowed in religious services and its use is even limited in private life. The Bedouins have evolved a rather monotonous chant accompanied by a one-string guitar and

A 14th-century enamelled oil lamp from a mosque is embellished with decorations of the type permitted by the Koran.

41

After the fast of Ramadan, friends and family gather for coffee and sweets. The fast lasts for one month, during which no food or drink is allowed during the daylight hours.

see each other for the first time during the marriage ceremony. Before the marriage is agreed upon, a dowry must be paid to the bride's family by either the prospective groom or his family. Some of the more modern, educated young people are breaking with these traditions and are choosing their own mates.

A man can divorce any of his four wives relatively easily, but not without certain obligations, such as providing for the children. It is much more difficult for a woman to secure a divorce. Although the Koran has many references to the rights and fair treatment of women, their position in all the traditional Arab societies is inferior.

Men and women rarely socialize together, and when families gather the women keep to themselves. Saudi women are generally required to wear veils in public and in the presence of strangers. They have been insulated from the social, business and political life of the country.

Only in recent years have women begun to emerge slowly to participate in some social and charitable activities—but they are still not allowed to drive cars! Social and cultural activi-

ties in which both sexes participate are virtually non-existent and while men often gather in coffee shops to smoke, gossip and drink innumerable cups of coffee, women's place is in the home or in women's clubs.

In fact, Saudi Arabian society is just beginning to organize for social, economic and

Foreigners and Saudis alike shop in supermarkets nowadays.

44

political purposes. The government permits associations or clubs for cultural and athletic purposes, and large gatherings are to be seen on religious occasions or at soccer games.

FOOD

The customary meal of the country consists of mutton roasted whole, served on a large platter with great heaps of rice, side dishes of eggplant roasted or fried, mixed green salad, eggs and cheese, and for dessert, fruit or a custard-like sweet with raisins or almonds. The bread is flat and round and is often large enough to be folded over several times. Originally one ate only with the right hand as the left hand was traditionally used for performing so-called "unclean functions."

Knives, spoons and forks are now coming into use. When they are not available, the diner dips his plate in the heap of rice and withdraws it

with the desired amount of food. Meat has to be broken by hand into pieces and vegetables scooped up with pieces of bread. Rice is squeezed with the fingers into small balls and dropped into the mouth. In the traditional manner, a host frequently selected choice bits of food and gave it to his guests. Both before and after meals, people wash their hands, after the meal usually with scented water. Once coffee is served, conversation stops—the meal is considered over, and the guests take their leave.

Alcoholic beverages are strictly forbidden and unavailable in Saudi Arabia and even visitors or foreigners working in the country are not allowed alcohol.

COFFEE

In Arabia, coffee is more than just a beverage, it is a social institution. Between meals, whenever two Arabs get together, coffee is served. It is very much a part of the Arabian scene— in fact it is believed that coffee originated in

Coffee beans are roasted over an open fire and then ground to a fine powder by mortar and pestle. Sometimes cardamom seeds or other spices are added to the coffee.

45

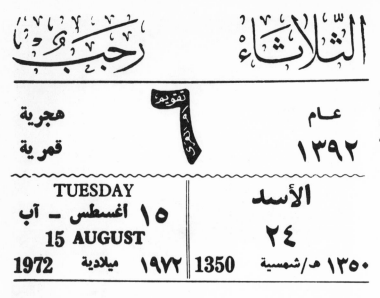

TELLING TIME

The task of telling time is not so simple in Saudi Arabia. The day officially begins at sunset. This means that night precedes daylight in the span of one full day. Thus Islamic noon (12 hours after the start of the new day) comes at approximately 6 o'clock in the morning, depending on the time of year, and on the time at which sunset takes place. The oil companies use daylight saving time and the domestic airlines use Greenwich time plus three hours as a form of compromise. One can purchase watches in Saudi Arabia which have two faces—one showing Greenwich, and the other, local (Islamic) time.

Saudi Arabia uses the Islamic calendar, which is dated from A.D. 622 when the prophet Mohammed fled from Mecca to Medina. Thus the first year of the Islamic calendar corresponds to A.D. 622 of the Gregorian calendar, and 1973, according to the Islamic calendar, is 1393.

The Islamic year is based on the lunar calendar, which has only $29\frac{1}{2}$ days in a month, therefore making the year 11 days shorter than the Gregorian year. Thus, an event or holy day based on the Islamic calendar takes place about 11 days earlier each successive year on the Gregorian calendar, causing events to revolve around the year—completing a cycle every 33 years. If the first day of Ramadan in 1972 was October 22, in 1973 it would be October 11, and in 1974, October 1, and so on until the full cycle of 33 years, at which time it would once again start on October 22. Therefore, according to the Islamic calendar the months have no permanent relation to the seasons.

*Crown Prince Fahd
receives a religious
dignitary.*

4. GOVERNMENT

SAUDI ARABIA is a monarchy with the Koran as the constitution. Executive and legislative authority is exercised by the King, who is chief of state and head of government. The council of ministers is appointed by and responsible to the King, who is also the supreme religious leader of the country.

The country functions on a framework of Arab tradition and Koranic (or Islamic) law called Sharia. The courts, whose magistrates are appointed by the Islamic leadership, are guided by the Sharia law, which is based entirely on the Koran. The Sharia is, in effect, the commentary and explanations added through the centuries by Islamic scholars to clarify and explain at greater length the basic points and rules set down in the Koran. Since the penal code is also based on the Koranic tenet of "an eye for an eye," the punishments meted out to offenders are at times quite cruel by Western standards.

Slavery was practiced on a wide scale until 1963, when it was officially made illegal by King Feisal.

Political parties or electors, in the Western sense, are unknown. Despite the rapid economic progress, the society remains conservative and religious. Although there is a total absence of representative government, there is a strong element of equality, which gives the individual certain rights, particularly the right to present grievances.

The country is divided into 18 administrative districts. Tribal and village leaders report and are responsible to the district governors, assuring a certain amount of central control in the remote areas. From 30 to 40 per cent of the population is organized on a tribal system. Each local tribe is headed by a sheikh and several tribes are grouped to form a main tribe headed by the paramount sheikh.

New housing in Dhahran reflects both Arabian and Western influence.

Late in 1974, King Feisal forced the 4 United States oil companies owning part of ARAMCO to agree to sell their remaining shares in the company to the Saudi government.

HOUSING

The settled people living in the oases and cities dwell in houses built of adobe and palm fronds. Wood is seldom seen, but galvanized steel and cement are being used more and more frequently. Prefabricated homes are becoming popular, particularly around oil installations where the oil companies assist the workers with loans. Due to the rapid influx of people to the cities, urban housing is still one of the main problems in spite of the great strides the government has made in this field.

SOCIAL WELFARE

Traditionally the family or tribe took care of its old, handicapped, and orphaned. However, due to the change from a tribal to an urban society, these traditional ways are disappearing. The government is trying to fill the void with improved health and welfare services. The oil companies have provided a good example— ARAMCO has an efficient plan for its employees that includes a pension fund, free medical care, and accident compensation.

The Saudi Government has established facilities for the housing and care of the old, disabled, and orphans. Presently these facilities can accommodate about 2,000 people. Other recent accomplishments include social service bureaus to advise people on social, cultural and agricultural problems. The first experimental bureau was established near Riyadh in 1960, with the help of United Nations specialists.

HEALTH

Saudi Arabia's chief health problems are typical of most other underdeveloped countries. Malnutrition was once widespread, resulting in anemia, scurvy and tuberculosis. Dysentery, trachoma, bilharzia (a worm infection) and typhoid are common. Since 1950, however, impressive improvements have taken place. It is one of the main goals of the government to provide the people with better health care.

A long-standing health problem has been the yearly influx of pilgrims, who frequently bring with them a variety of communicable diseases. New health care facilities are planned to serve both the Saudi citizens and the pilgrims. There are 47 hospitals with a total of 6,926 beds, 531 clinics, and 325 health units, of which 23 are mobile units that regularly tour the remote parts of the country.

Strict laws have now been enacted to curb communicable diseases. Immunization is being offered throughout the country and special mobile teams are regularly inspecting water and sewer systems. Various U.N. agencies have assisted in the establishment of medical facilities with particular attention to preventive medicine.

Outside of Riyadh a vast medical complex has been built—King Faisal Medical City. Opened in 1975, the complex is roughly equivalent to seven conventional hospitals, and boasts equipment and technology that are the equal of any in the world.

The main entrance of the international departure section at the beautifully designed Dhahran Air Terminal appears deserted. Actually, the airport is one of the busiest in the country and handles large jets.

5. THE ECONOMY

IN RECENT years Saudi Arabia has had an average economic growth of 9 per cent annually. The greatest single factor of economic importance is oil. Production is constantly increasing, and in 1977 it reached 38,214,000 metric tons per month. Saudi Arabia is one of the largest producers in the world, and with proven reserves of 150,000,000,000 barrels, it has one of the largest reserves. In 1972, it replaced Venezuela as the world's largest exporter of oil. Oil royalties account for more than 85 per cent of the nation's total revenue. More than 90 per cent of the oil is produced by ARAMCO.

OIL DEVELOPMENT

The country is rapidly expanding and diversifying its industrial potential through the use of income derived from the petroleum industry. The government is also developing its own petroleum industry, including refining and marketing facilities. With the assistance of several international firms, exploration for oil is also being planned in the central part of the country—an area relatively unexplored so far.

Offshore oil developments are also being extended. To facilitate this, ARAMCO is putting

To facilitate and speed up the loading of oil aboard tankers, the oil companies are installing "Sea Islands," which enable many huge tankers to take on oil simultaneously. This picture shows a model of ARAMCO's *Sea Island IV*, with a tower crane in the middle, an elevated control house behind it, loading arms at both ends, and multi-purpose towers at the corners.

Sea Island IV was placed in position on June 27, 1972. In this view the legs have been lowered to the sea bottom and are being driven in by crane-hung pile drivers.

The control house of ARAMCO's Sea Island IV was installed in an inlet of the independent Gulf island of Bahrain, and its eight legs inserted and lowered 24 feet into the water. The structure was then towed from this location to waters off the Ras Tanura Marine Terminal, where it became a part of the company's growing offshore oil-loading facilities.

into operation a gigantic floating storage vessel. Anchored off shore, moored to a single buoy in water about 130 feet deep, the vessel has a storage capacity of 1,800,000 barrels and is capable of taking in and discharging crude oil simultaneously.

Much Saudi oil is shipped by tankers to Europe and Japan to be refined, although some of it is now being refined in Saudi Arabia—there is a huge refinery operated by ARAMCO at Ras Tanura. Some of the oil is shipped by tankers to the Red Sea port of Jiddah, where a new refinery has been constructed. Some is carried by pipelines to the island of Bahrain, and some through another pipeline to the Mediterranean.

Ras Tanura is the largest oil shipping port on the Persian Gulf. The huge tanks are used to store the oil until it is loaded aboard tankers for shipment to refineries.

In an ARAMCO storage yard, an air-supported warehouse holds medical supplies.

ARAMCO

The Arabian American Oil Company began as a United States holding company, and was one of the largest single United States investments abroad. ARAMCO has played a very important rôle in the development of Saudi Arabia. In 1933, when the first concession was granted to ARAMCO the country was a primitive tribal society and it was the discovery of oil and its development by ARAMCO that created the need for new roads, jobs, airfields and housing.

Much of the country was explored and mapped for the first time by ARAMCO engineers.

The influence of ARAMCO has been also quite impressive in providing technical training and in the field of social services by providing its workers with benefits unheard of in Saudi Arabia—housing, health, insurance and recreation facilities.

WATER AND ELECTRICITY

One of the greatest problems is lack of water, and due to this scarcity only about 15 per cent of the land is arable. To combat this problem

An ARAMCO technician adjusts a multiple valve called a "Christmas Tree," atop an oil well in Dhahran. In the background is a mosque built for the Muslim employees of the company.

Tankers line the loading piers at Ras Tanura terminal.

the government has enlisted the help of the FAO (the U.N. Food and Agricultural Organization) to help in irrigation projects and water conservation. Several small dams have been constructed, and in 1971 the government signed a contract with an Italian firm to build a large dam at Abha, in the south.

A huge water desalinization plant has been set up at Jiddah with a daily capacity of 5,000,000 gallons (190,000,000 litres), and another has been built in the east.

The largest industry after oil is the production of electricity. Presently there are six large plants supplying electricity to the major cities. There are also small generating plants throughout the country. All the generating plants use diesel engines, thus enabling them to utilize the plentiful local oil as fuel.

ARAMCO has several industrial training facilities to educate workers in the various skills needed. This is the training shop for basic and specialized manual skills.

The airport terminal in Jiddah which receives pilgrims from as far away as Morocco and Indonesia, is too close to the city to allow for expansion. It is being replaced by a new one, which will be the largest in the world.

general area. Work is being done to reactivate the famous Hejaz railway, in order to provide rail communication with Jordan and Syria. This railway has been out of service since World War I. Maintained by the Turks as their main supply line for their occupation of Hejaz, it became a primary target of the raiders organized by Lawrence of Arabia and the forces of Hussein, Emir of Mecca.

AVIATION

Saudi Arabia has a large fleet of commercial aircraft, ranging from DC-3's to modern jets. The main airports at Jiddah, Dhahran and Riyadh are capable of handling the huge modern jets, while the other smaller airports form an important link in the country's growing transportation network. Saudi Arabian Airlines, a government-owned company, flies to North Africa, Beirut, London, Rome, Milan, Paris, Amsterdam, Geneva, and Frankfurt.

Travelling by air in Saudi Arabia gives one an excellent opportunity to see the traditional and the modern side by side—for instance, a desert

sheikh accompanied by an attendant sitting next to an American engineer. Planes now land on airfields where until a few years ago roads did not even exist.

Near Jiddah, Saudi Arabia is building the world's largest airport. Scheduled to open in 1982, the airport covers an area of 41 square miles (107 sq km), nearly twice the size of the island of Manhattan, or nearly as large as the island of Jersey.

CURRENCY

For many years the country did not have paper currency, in fact the law specifically forbade the printing and use of paper money. All

Saudi Arabian banknotes—official paper currency—were issued for the first time in 1961. Until then paper money was officially called "pilgrim's receipts." The banknote on the top is worth 100 riyals and the one on the bottom, 50 riyals.

60

transactions were carried out with silver, gold or with foreign currency.

To facilitate matters, in 1953, the Saudi government issued a paper currency called "pilgrim's receipts." Officially the purpose was to relieve the pilgrims of the necessity of carrying large quantities of silver and gold. However, it proved to be so successful that it was gradually adopted for all transactions. In 1961, the government formally issued a new official paper currency and in 1963 the pilgrim's money went out of circulation.

COMMUNICATIONS

TELEVISION AND RADIO

Television and radio are the primary sources of entertainment, and there were 10 television and 20 radio stations in 1977. The offerings are varied, consisting of educational broadcasts, readings from the Koran, and Egyptian "soap operas." The voice of a Saudi woman was heard for the first time on the radio in 1963, and since then women are playing a more prominent rôle in radio and television.

PRESS

There are 11 daily newspapers and 15 newspapers and magazines that appear weekly or monthly. The magazines range from popular pictorials to literary and scientific reviews.

Most of the newspapers are privately owned, but are subsidized through government advertising and special tax privileges. The government keeps an eye on the press and, although there is no direct censorship, newspapers are expected to refrain from publishing anything offensive to the state. Attacks or criticisms on the institution of the monarchy are not permitted.

Typesetters are at work at the Al Mutawa Press in Dammam, where both Arabic and English publications are printed.

This photograph shows the construction in Mecca of a hotel, mosque, and conference hall complex, supervised by European architects. As non-Muslims are forbidden in Mecca, the European architects and supervisors followed the progress of the construction from a distance of 10 miles (16 km) via closed-circuit television cameras.

TOURISM

Tourism is undeveloped. Visitors are allowed to enter the country by applying for special permission from the Ministry of Foreign Affairs. Journalists are admitted by special invitation of the government. Employees of oil companies and other firms conducting business in Saudi Arabia can secure permission more easily. The holy cities of Mecca and Medina are forbidden to non-Muslims.

A trend towards improved tourist facilities was launched in June, 1974, when a modern Inter-Continental Hotel opened in Riyadh. Similar hotels were opened in Jiddah and Dhahran.

The Saudi Arabian Government railway, which went into operation in 1951, spans the 375 miles (600 km) from Dammam to Riyadh.

Dammam fishermen lay their fish traps in the shallow waters of the Arabian Gulf. Fishing along the coast is an important source of protein.

A date grower in Qatif Oasis climbs to the top of a tall, graceful date palm to gather the ripening fruit.

INDEX